D1088628

BUILDING BY DESIGN

ENGINEERING
THE COLOSSEUM

BY YVETTE LAPIERRE

CONTENT CONSULTANT
Lynne C. Lancaster
Professor, Department of Classics and World Religions
Ohio University

Core Library

An Imprint of Abdo Publishing
abdopublishing.com

Cover image: The Colosseum has stood in the city of
Rome for nearly 2,000 years.

abdopublishing.com

Published by Abdo Publishing, a division of ABDO, PO Box 398166,
Minneapolis, Minnesota 55439. Copyright © 2018 by Abdo Consulting
Group, Inc. International copyrights reserved in all countries. No part of this
book may be reproduced in any form without written permission from the
publisher. Core Library™ is a trademark and logo of Abdo Publishing.

Printed in the United States of America, North Mankato, Minnesota
052017
092017

THIS BOOK CONTAINS
RECYCLED MATERIALS

Cover Photo: Shutterstock Images
Interior Photos: Shutterstock Images, 1; Dea Picture Library/De Agostini/Getty Images, 4–5;
Ann Ronan Pictures/Print Collector/Hulton Archive/Getty Images, 8, 31; Georg Gerster/Science
Source, 10, 43; Culture Club/Hulton Archive/Getty Images, 12–13; iStockphoto, 15, 17, 45;
DigitalGlobe/ScapeWare3d/Getty Images, 18 (left); DigitalGlobe/Getty Images News/Getty
Images, 18 (right); Dea/G. Nimatallah/De Agostini/Getty Images, 20; Bucchi Francesco/Shutterstock
Images, 22–23; Beyhan Yazar/iStockphoto, 24–25; Merve Karahan/iStockphoto, 27; De Agostini
Picture Library/De Agostini/Getty Images, 29; S. Borisov/iStockphoto, 34–35; Science & Society
Picture Library/SSPL/Getty Images, 37; Andrew Medichini/AP Images, 38–39

Editor: Heidi Schoof
Imprint Designer: Maggie Villaume
Series Design Direction: Laura Polzin

Publisher's Cataloging-in-Publication Data

Names: LaPierre, Yvette, author.
Title: Engineering the Colosseum / by Yvette LaPierre.
Description: Minneapolis, MN : Abdo Publishing, 2018. | Series: Building by
    design | Includes bibliographical references and index.
Identifiers: LCCN 2017930242 | ISBN 9781532111648 (lib. bdg.) |
    ISBN 9781680789492 (ebook)
Subjects: LCSH: Structural engineering--Miscellanea--Juvenile literature. |
    Colosseum (Rome, Italy)--Design and construction--Juvenile literature. | Civil
    engineering--Juvenile literature. | Buildings, structures, etc.-- Juvenile
    literature. | Buildings--Miscellanea--Juvenile literature.
Classification: DDC 624--dc23
LC record available at http://lccn.loc.gov/2017930242

CONTENTS

LET THE GAMES BEGIN

Two men faced each other in the ring. Thousands of people cheered around them. Both men wore armor. They carried shields and weapons. They fought long and hard. Finally, one staggered and fell to the ground. The fallen gladiator looked up to the audience. He heard the crowd roar. Would he live to fight another day? Or would he be killed? He waited for the emperor to decide his fate.

Gladiator contests were a regular part of Roman life. People crowded into arenas

Gladiator fights were fierce, brutal contests.

to watch these fights and other events. In the mornings were the wild animal hunts. Animals such as bears, lions, and elephants were hunted or made to fight each other. Criminals were executed at midday. The high point of the day was the gladiator bouts in the afternoons. Pairs of gladiators fought for their lives. Most gladiators were convicts, slaves, or prisoners of war. The greatest venue for the games was Rome's Colosseum.

THE FLAVIAN AMPHITHEATER

The city of Rome was the center of a vast and powerful empire. At its height, it controlled lands from Britain to the Middle East. The first Roman emperor was Augustus. He took power in 31 BCE. Citizens trusted him. To show his strength and reward his people, he organized arena games.

Not all of his successors were popular. Nero became emperor in 54 CE. Ten years later, a fire burned much of central Rome. It left thousands of people homeless. Nero did not rebuild the homes. Instead, he took the land for himself. He built a lavish palace there. It was surrounded by a private park. The park included an artificial lake. A statue of Nero stood at the entrance. Ancient authors claim it was about 120 feet (36.5 m) tall.

Vespasian became the next emperor in 69 CE. He knew he needed to regain the people's trust. He opened the palace and the park to the public. Where Nero's lake stood, he decided to build the world's

A statue from the 50s CE shows the head of Nero.

largest amphitheater. There he would stage the greatest games ever. The amphitheater would return the land to the citizens. It would also be an opportunity to demonstrate the empire's power.

Work on the amphitheater began in 72 CE. Opening ceremonies were held under Vespasian's eldest son, Titus, in 80 CE. When finished, the huge oval structure was four stories high. It covered six acres (2.4 ha) of land. Eighty entrances ringed the ground floor. According to ancient texts, the building could seat 87,000 people. At the time of its construction, it was called the Flavian Amphitheater. It later took on the name *Colosseum*.

The Colosseum is famous for being the place where people and animals were killed for entertainment. This can make it difficult or disturbing to enjoy the Colosseum

NAMING THE COLOSSEUM

The original name for the Colosseum was the Flavian Amphitheater. It was named after Vespasian's family, the Flavians. By the Middle Ages (500–1500 CE), it was known as the Colosseum. The source may be the statue of Nero. Vespasian left the huge statue, or *Colossus Neronis,* standing. He replaced Nero's head on the statue with the head of a god and renamed it.

The Colosseum still stands today as one of the best-known structures from the ancient world.

today. But the building itself can be appreciated as a triumph of planning and engineering. It continues to influence modern builders.

STRAIGHT TO THE
SOURCE

The Roman poet Martial wrote *Liber de Spectaculis*. This collection of short verses celebrated the opening of the Flavian Amphitheater in 80 CE. In it, he describes the monument:

> *Where the starry Colossus sees the constellations at close range and lofty scaffolding rises in the middle of the road, once gleamed the odious halls of a cruel monarch, and in all Rome there stood a single house. Where rises before our eyes the august pile of the Amphitheatre, was once Nero's lake. Where we admire the warm baths, a speedy gift, a haughty tract of land had robbed the poor of their dwellings.*

> Source: Janet Huskinson. *Experiencing Rome: Culture, Identity and Power in the Roman Empire*. London: Routledge, 2000. Print. 80.

Consider Your Audience

This verse was written almost 2,000 years ago. Consider how you would adapt it for a modern audience, such as your parents, your principal, or younger friends. Write a blog post conveying this same information for the new audience. How does your new approach differ from the original text, and why?

PREPARING TO BUILD

Before beginning to build, Vespasian and his architects had to agree on the location and general design. Amphitheaters were not new to Rome. But most of the earlier ones were simple wooden arenas. They were often built for festivals. They would be taken down after the games were over.

The general design of most amphitheaters was an oval arena surrounded by tiers of seating. This design provided plenty of seating that people could get to quickly. Every seat offered a good view.

Smaller amphitheaters had long been in use in Rome.

The building that Vespasian envisioned was one of a kind. He intended to build a permanent stone amphitheater. It would be the largest in the world. Its size and complexity would require the very latest in Roman engineering and materials.

PERSPECTIVES
VITRUVIUS

The identity of the Colosseum's architect is unknown. In addition, there are no written records of how it was designed and built. But undoubtedly, its designer would have been familiar with the work of Marcus Vitruvius Pollio. Vitruvius was one of the most important Roman architects of his day. He wrote *De Architectura*, or *On Architecture*, around 15 BCE. This is the oldest known work about the theory of building. According to Vitruvius, buildings should always be beautiful, stable, and useful.

The site chosen for the Flavian Amphitheater was in the center of town. Vespasian signaled that he was returning the land to the people. The building was to be built on the site of Nero's lake. The lake would have to be

The travertine walls of the Colosseum have been damaged over time.

drained. Nero had built an aqueduct to carry water into his artificial lake. To drain it, the builders cut this supply of water.

MATERIALS

The three main materials used in the Colosseum were travertine, tuff, and concrete. Builders also used bricks and about 300 short tons (272 metric tons) of iron clamps.

Travertine is a type of limestone. Roman builders valued it because it was strong. More than 3,500,000 cubic feet (100,000 cubic m) of travertine was brought to the site. Barges and ox-carts carried the material from outside Rome. Tuff, or volcanic stone, was common all around Rome. It is softer and lighter than travertine. However, it is still strong enough to be a building material.

Concrete consists of small stones, or

GRADING MATERIALS

The designers of the Colosseum chose the right materials for the job. More importantly, they knew where to use which materials. Engineers know that any point in a structure must support the weight of everything above it. The heaviest stones and materials were used in the lower portions of the building. These were the strongest materials. The builders used the lighter materials at the top. This is known as grading. The practice is still used by builders today.

A sturdy underground foundation supports the massive weight of the Colosseum.

aggregate, held together with mortar. It had been in use for nearly three centuries. By the 100s BCE, Romans invented a new kind of mortar to use for concrete. They used fine-grained volcanic ash instead of sand. When

THE COLOSSEUM VERSUS MODERN STADIUMS

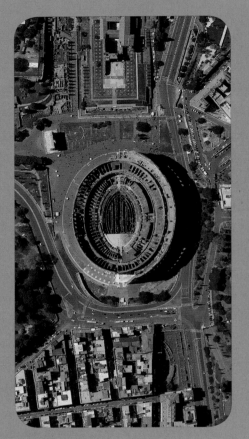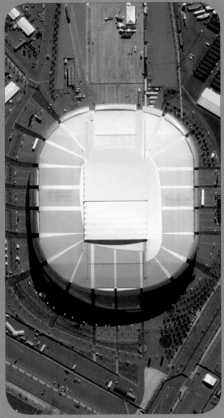

These images show the Colosseum in modern times and a modern football stadium at the same scale. How do the sizes of these two venues differ? What are the reasons for this? How do the parts of the cities shown around the stadiums differ?

mixed with lime and water, it produced a much stronger

mortar. It would harden even in wet conditions. Roman

concrete was inexpensive and easy to use. It helped make the Colosseum possible.

FOUNDATION

One of the greatest challenges of this massive building was its great weight. It would need to rest on a very solid foundation. After draining Nero's lake, workers dug a vast oval trench for the foundation. The trench was nearly 20 feet (6 m) deep. It was dug entirely by hand. This took at least a year.

Next, the workers built two walls in the oval trench. One was inside the other. The outer wall followed the edge of the trench. Each wall was almost 10 feet (3 m) thick and 41 feet (12.5 m) high. Both walls were made of concrete and faced with brick. The gap between the two walls was filled with concrete. This enormous donut of concrete would distribute the building's weight evenly. It would keep it from sinking into the ground.

The foundation was divided into four areas by tunnels. One tunnel ran the length of the oval from end

to end. The other ran side to side. Drains ran under the tunnels and sloped outward. The system of drains would collect rainwater. This would keep the arena dry when the building was completed. The Colosseum still stands today because the foundation was so well built. This was one of the greatest achievements of its engineers.

EXPLORE ONLINE

Chapter Two discusses the materials and techniques used in the construction of the Colosseum. A recent restoration project of the Colosseum has revealed much about the original construction. The website below details the project with maps, photos, and videos. As you know, every source is different. How is the information given in the website different from the information in this chapter? What information is the same? What new information did you learn from the website?

THE COLOSSEUM RESTORED
abdocorelibrary.com/engineering-the-colosseum

The Colosseum's drainage system has helped the structure continue standing for many centuries.

BUILDING THE COLOSSEUM

The foundation was finished. Now it was time to start building the heavy structure that would sit on its sturdy walls.

Vespasian was eager to finish the amphitheater quickly. To speed construction, the structure was divided into sections. Crews of skilled laborers worked on each of the sections. There are slight differences in the sections. This suggests that each crew followed the same basic plan but worked independently.

With the foundation complete, work on the huge main structure of the Colosseum could begin.

The well-built arches of the Colosseum have supported the structure for centuries.

The building had to be strong enough to support floors of stone seating. But it couldn't be solid. It needed plenty of openings to allow people to flow through the building. How could this be done? The answer was the arch.

ARCHES AND VAULTS

An arch is a curved structure that spans a space. Arches support great weight and make buildings stronger. Romans combined arches to form ceilings called barrel vaults. A series of arches supported by columns makes an arcade.

Arches can support more weight than flat beams can. Rather than all the weight pressing down on a single point, the shape of the arch distributes the weight. The force travels across the rounded top and down the supporting sides. A strong passage is created underneath.

Romans did not invent arches. People had built them from stone and brick for centuries. Romans were, however, the first to use concrete to make arches. The result was strong yet lightweight vaults. Concrete vaults in the Colosseum resulted in a sturdy building that was easy to enter and exit. Concrete, vaults, and arches made the Colosseum possible.

THE CAVEA

The basic design of the Colosseum is a series of ovals leading in from the outside wall to the arena in the center. Vaulted tunnels ran through the basement

Tourists today still use the ground-level entrances built by the Colosseum's original engineers.

below the arena. They were used by the gladiators.

Wild animals and their handlers also used these spaces.

Trapdoors around the arena's wooden floor allowed

props and animals to appear in the arena as if by magic. The floor was covered with sand. The sand kept the fighters from slipping. It also soaked up blood. The Latin word for "sand" is *harena*. That is where the modern word *arena* comes from.

Engineers designed the Colosseum to allow many people to move through it easily. Each level of the seating area, or *cavea*, rose in tiers around the arena. The outside of each level was built of strong travertine arcades. The arcade at the ground level included 80 entrances. Seventy-six of the entrances were numbered for the general public.

CROSS SECTION OF THE COLOSSEUM

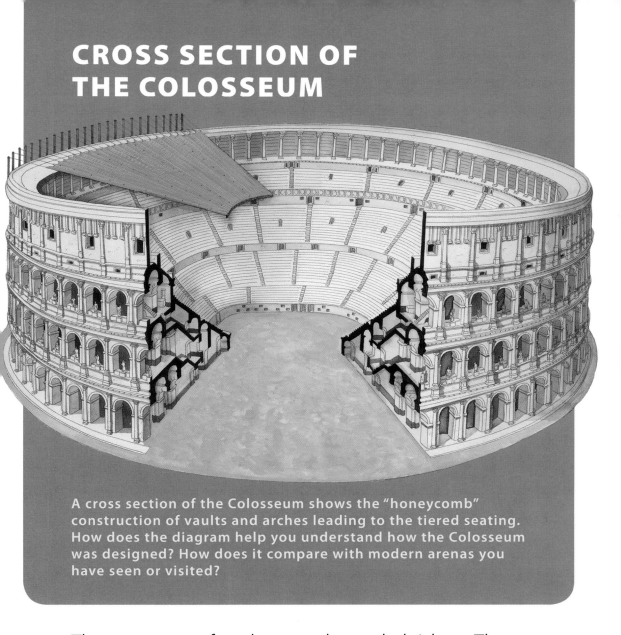

A cross section of the Colosseum shows the "honeycomb" construction of vaults and arches leading to the tiered seating. How does the diagram help you understand how the Colosseum was designed? How does it compare with modern arenas you have seen or visited?

The games were free, but people needed tickets. The tickets told them which entrance to use and where to sit. Arches and vaults led to corridors and staircases in each level. Each level was divided into sections of seating. Each section had its own staircase. The vaulted passages and stairways to the seating areas were called the *vomitoria*. Each arched entrance had a number carved above it. The number was matched to the ticket. The cavea was so well planned that the entire audience could leave the building in minutes.

LATER CHANGES

The Colosseum builders worked quickly. Still, the amphitheater was not quite finished when Vespasian died in 79 CE. His oldest son, Titus Flavius, completed the final level of seating a year later. Titus also added a huge canvas awning, called a *velarium*. It protected people from the sun and rain. Scholars do not agree on exactly how it worked. It may have stretched over a network of ropes tied to posts along the top of the building. The supports for these posts can still be seen along the exterior of the structure.

An efficient design allowed audience members to move quickly through the Colosseum.

NAUMACHIA

Roman writers described mock naval battles, or *naumachia*, held at arenas, including the Colosseum. But was it possible to flood the basement? The Colosseum was built to drain water, not hold it in. The foundation floor and drain pipes sloped outward. Scholars believe the aqueduct for Nero's lake could have flooded the arena. And traces of mortar used for waterproofing have been found on basement walls. Also, there is evidence that the original arena floor was a removable wooden one. It may have been removed at times to allow for flooding. But Domitian's permanent basement walls would have made flooding the arena impossible.

Titus sponsored 100 days of opening games. These included wild animal fights, staged hunting, and gladiator battles. Some claim that 5,000 animals were killed in one day. Accounts also describe mock sea battles staged on the flooded arena.

Vespasian's second son, Domitian, made big changes to the basement. He built a complex system of permanent rooms and tunnels called the *hypogeum*. Later, elevators on pulley systems were also added. They lifted fighters, caged animals, and scenery to the arena floor. Large, hinged platforms allowed animals to walk up to the arena. Underground tunnels connected the hypogeum to nearby barracks for gladiators.

At its opening, the Colosseum looked very different than it does now. The cream-colored travertine surface was clean and polished. Statues lined the outer archways. Inside, the amphitheater was brightly painted. It was decorated with statues and fountains.

FURTHER EVIDENCE

Chapter Three provides information about how Roman engineers used arches to build the Colosseum. Identify the chapter's main points about arches. Watch the video on the website below. Does the information in the video help you understand better how arches support the weight of the Colosseum? Does it offer new information?

ENGINEERING THE IMPOSSIBLE: THE COLOSSEUM
abdocorelibrary.com/engineering-the-colosseum

THE COLOSSEUM TODAY

The Colosseum continued to host gladiator games and animal hunts for centuries. These large events showed the empire's power. But as the Roman Empire weakened, so did the Colosseum.

DECLINE

In the centuries following the building of the Colosseum, the Roman Empire struggled to defend its borders. Its wars were costly. Less money was available to keep up the arena for large games. Gladiator shows ended in the

The Colosseum now sits among modern buildings in Rome.

PROPHECY

In the 700s CE, the Venerable Bede, an English monk and historian, wrote, "When falls the Coliseum, Rome shall fall." This well-known prophecy may refer to the building. Or Bede may have meant the statue of Nero. The Colossus did eventually fall, as did the Roman Empire. But the amphitheater still stands.

430s CE. However, smaller animal hunts continued.

The Roman Empire finally fell in 476 CE. The Colosseum slowly declined into ruin. Fires swept through it. Earthquakes shook it. The quakes knocked down entire walls. People used the building for planting vegetable gardens, stabling animals, and dumping trash. But mostly it was used as a source of materials for new buildings. People hauled away travertine blocks by the cartload. Even the lead pipes and iron clamps were taken. In the mid-1600s, the local government finally realized it had to put a stop to this. Otherwise, nothing would be left of the Colosseum.

The earliest photographs of the Colosseum, dating to the mid-1800s, show the structure much as it appears today.

RESTORATION

Despite all that damage, the Colosseum still stands today. It is Italy's most popular monument. Millions visit it every year. Centuries of neglect, failed attempts to rebuild, and pollution, however, have taken their toll on the building.

Workers scrub the Colosseum's walls in July 2016.

A restoration project is underway. Archaeologists, architects, engineers, and restorers are at work on the building. The goal is to return the neglected monument to its former glory.

The first stage of the project was completed in the summer of 2016. Workers carefully scrubbed centuries of soot and grime from the walls. Others repaired stone and brickwork. They worked on one section at a time.

That way the monument could stay open to visitors. The original cream-colored travertine stone can now be seen. The next step was to restore the hypogeum.

THE COLOSSEUM LIGHTS UP LIFE

Since 1999, the Colosseum has been used to protest the death penalty. The campaign is supported by the Italian government and other groups. When a government somewhere in the world stops using the death penalty, golden light shines on the monument. The Colosseum now is a place of life rather than death.

Roman officials plan to hold large cultural events in the Colosseum. That should be possible, architects say, because the building is still structurally sound. This is a testament to the remarkable engineering of the Colosseum nearly 2,000 years ago.

STRAIGHT TO THE
SOURCE

In 1818, the English poet Percy Bysshe Shelley visited the Colosseum and described it in a letter:

> The Coliseum is unlike any work of human hands I ever saw before. It is of enormous height and circuit, and the arches built of massy stones are piled on one another and jut into the blue air, shattered into the forms of overhanging rocks. It has been changed by time into the image of an amphitheatre of rocky hills overgrown by the wild olive, the myrtle, and the fig-tree, and threaded by little paths, which wind among its ruined stairs and immeasurable galleries. . . . But a small part of the exterior circumference remains—it is exquisitely light and beautiful. . . . The interior is all ruin.

Source: Percy Bysshe Shelley. *Essays, Letters from Abroad, Translations and Fragments*. Mrs. Shelley, ed. London: Edward Moxon, Dover Street, 1845. Print. 118–119.

Point of View

Compare this description of the Colosseum to the poet Martial's in Chapter One. What is the point of view of each author? How do they differ in their descriptions of the Colosseum, and why? Write a short essay comparing the two points of view reflected in the primary sources in this book.

- ...egan in 72 CE, and the ...J CE.

- ...gest Roman amphitheater ever ...or more people.

- ...ches made the Colosseum possible.

- The Co... ...d 157 feet (48 m) high. It was more than 620 feet (1... ...ong and 512 (156 m) wide and covered 6 acres (2.4 ha). The arena inside measured 262 feet (80 m) long and 177 feet (54 m) wide.

- More than 1 million short tons (900,000 metric tons) of travertine limestone, concrete, brick, and volcanic stone were used in its construction.

- Gladiator battles in the Colosseum ended in the mid-430s CE.

- Four million people visit the Colosseum every year.

- The restoration of the Colosseum was expected to cost 25 million euros ($35 million).

STOP AND THINK

Say What?

Studying ancient Roman architecture can mean learning a lot of new vocabulary. Find five words in this book you had never heard before. Use a dictionary to find out what they mean. Then write the meanings in your own words and use each word in a new sentence.

You Are There

Millions of people visit the Colosseum every year. Imagine you are visiting the monument. Write a letter to friends or family about your visit. What are you seeing? What events from the past can you see in the structure today? Be sure to add plenty of detail.

Dig Deeper

After reading this book, what questions do you still have about the Colosseum? With an adult's help, find a few reliable sources that can help you answer your questions. Write a paragraph about what you learned.

Take a Stand

In Chapter Four, you read Percy Bysshe Shelley's account of his visit to the Colosseum in 1818. He found beauty in the ruins. Other writers, including Charles Dickens, have expressed the same opinion. Do you think the ruins of a building can be more beautiful or more interesting than the original building? What do you think about restoring the Colosseum?

GLOSSARY

amphitheater
an oval building with tiers of seats around an open area for games or performances

architecture
the art or science of designing and creating buildings

arena
the central area in an amphitheater where the entertainment takes place

colossus
an unusually large and impressive statue

empire
a group of countries or territories ruled by a single person

gladiator
a man in ancient Rome who fought as public entertainment

republic
a form of government that allows people to elect officials

restoration
the process of returning something to its former condition by cleaning and repairing it

LEARN
MORE

Books

James, Simon. *Ancient Rome.* New York: DK, 2015.

O'Connor, Jim. *Where Is the Colosseum?* New York: Grosset & Dunlap, 2017.

Rose, Simon. *Colosseum.* New York: AV2 by Weigl Publishers, 2013.

Websites

To learn more about Building by Design, visit **abdobooklinks.com**. These links are routinely monitored and updated to provide the most current information available.

Visit **abdocorelibrary.com** for free additional tools for teachers and students.

INDEX

About the Author

Yvette LaPierre lives in North Dakota with her family, two dogs, and a crested gecko. She writes and edits books and articles for children and adults. She enjoys visiting the ruins of historic buildings.